WRITERS ON TASK

FOCUS YOUR WRITING TASKS & KEEP MOVING FORWARD

Denise Hartzler

Published by Look Up Publications, LLC in 2020
First Edition: First Printing

Design, Cover, and Writing © 2020 Denise Hartzler

www.denisehartzler.com

All rights reserved. No part of this book may be reproduced or transmistted in any form or by any means, including but not limited to information storage and retrieval systems, electronic, mechanical, photocopy, recording, etc. without written permission from the copyright holder.

ISBN: 978-1-7346070-0-0

Writing is a life-long journey meant to be shared.

How to use this book

Writing is a long journey and feels overwhelming at times, but it is a journey worth taking.

Studies have shown that if you take an enormous task, like writing a book, and break it down into smaller tasks, you will have a higher rate of success.

The purpose of this book is to help you break down all the various pieces of writing a story that have you feeling overwhelmed or stuck.

In this journal, you will circle a specific task related to your writing project. Once you know what you are working on, it's time to concentrate. Warm your brain up with an open space, then use the remaining lined pages to write.

By taking a few moments to focus your mind on that one little task, you will find yourself making forward progress with your writing goals.

Writers on Task

Today I will focus on:

Brainstorming   Researching   Outlining

Character Sketch   Setting   Dialogue

Scene(s)   POV   Plot

Revisions/Edits   Synopsis   Pitch

Other: _____

Writers on Task

Today I will focus on:

Brainstorming   Researching   Outlining

Character Sketch   Setting   Dialoge

Scene(s)   POV   Plot

Revisions/Edits   Synopsis   Pitch

Other: _____

Writers on Task

Today I will focus on:

Brainstorming   Researching   Outlining

Character Sketch   Setting   Dialoge

Scene(s)   POV   Plot

Revisions/Edits   Synopsis   Pitch

Other: _____

Writers on Task

Today I will focus on:

Brainstorming	Researching	Outlining

Character Sketch	Setting	Dialoge

Scene(s)	POV	Plot

Revisions/Edits	Synopsis	Pitch

Other: _____

Writers on Task

Today I will focus on:

Brainstorming   Researching   Outlining

Character Sketch   Setting   Dialoge

Scene(s)   POV   Plot

Revisions/Edits   Synopsis   Pitch

Other: _____

Writers on Task

Today I will focus on:

Brainstorming	Researching	Outlining

Character Sketch	Setting	Dialoge

Scene(s)	POV	Plot

Revisions/Edits	Synopsis	Pitch

Other: _____

Writers on Task

Today I will focus on:

Brainstorming	Researching	Outlining

Character Sketch	Setting	Dialoge

Scene(s)	POV	Plot

Revisions/Edits	Synopsis	Pitch

Other: _____

Writers on Task

Today I will focus on:

Brainstorming | Researching | Outlining

Character Sketch | Setting | Dialoge

Scene(s) | POV | Plot

Revisions/Edits | Synopsis | Pitch

Other: _____

Writers on Task

Today I will focus on:

Brainstorming   Researching   Outlining

Character Sketch   Setting   Dialoge

Scene(s)   POV   Plot

Revisions/Edits   Synopsis   Pitch

Other: _____

Writers on Task

Today I will focus on:

Brainstorming　　　Researching　　　Outlining

Character Sketch　　Setting　　　　　Dialoge

Scene(s)　　　　　　POV　　　　　　Plot

Revisions/Edits　　　Synopsis　　　　Pitch

Other: _____

Writers on Task

Today I will focus on:

Brainstorming

Character Sketch

Scene(s)

Revisions/Edits

Researching

Setting

POV

Synopsis

Outlining

Dialoge

Plot

Pitch

Other: _____

Writers on Task

Today I will focus on:

Brainstorming   Researching   Outlining

Character Sketch   Setting   Dialoge

Scene(s)   POV   Plot

Revisions/Edits   Synopsis   Pitch

Other: _____

Writers on Task

Today I will focus on:

Brainstorming

Character Sketch

Scene(s)

Revisions/Edits

Researching

Setting

POV

Synopsis

Outlining

Dialoge

Plot

Pitch

Other: _____

Writers on Task

Today I will focus on:

Brainstorming   Researching   Outlining

Character Sketch   Setting   Dialoge

Scene(s)   POV   Plot

Revisions/Edits   Synopsis   Pitch

Other: _____

Writers on Task

Today I will focus on:

Brainstorming   Researching   Outlining

Character Sketch   Setting   Dialoge

Scene(s)   POV   Plot

Revisions/Edits   Synopsis   Pitch

Other: _____

Writers on Task

Today I will focus on:

Brainstorming　　　　Researching　　　　Outlining

Character Sketch　　　Setting　　　　　　Dialogue

Scene(s)　　　　　　　POV　　　　　　　Plot

Revisions/Edits　　　　Synopsis　　　　　Pitch

Other: _____

Writers on Task

Today I will focus on:

Brainstorming	Researching	Outlining

Character Sketch	Setting	Dialoge

Scene(s)	POV	Plot

Revisions/Edits	Synopsis	Pitch

Other: _____

Writers on Task

Today I will focus on:

Brainstorming Researching Outlining

Character Sketch Setting Dialoge

Scene(s) POV Plot

Revisions/Edits Synopsis Pitch

Other: _____

Writers on Task

Today I will focus on:

Brainstorming

Character Sketch

Scene(s)

Revisions/Edits

Other: _____

Researching

Setting

POV

Synopsis

Outlining

Dialoge

Plot

Pitch

Writers on Task

Today I will focus on:

Brainstorming

Character Sketch

Scene(s)

Revisions/Edits

Other: _____

Researching

Setting

POV

Synopsis

Outlining

Dialoge

Plot

Pitch

Writers on Task

Today I will focus on:

Brainstorming

Researching

Outlining

Character Sketch

Setting

Dialoge

Scene(s)

POV

Plot

Revisions/Edits

Synopsis

Pitch

Other: _____

Writers on Task

Today I will focus on:

Brainstorming   Researching   Outlining

Character Sketch   Setting   Dialoge

Scene(s)   POV   Plot

Revisions/Edits   Synopsis   Pitch

Other: _____

Writers on Task

Today I will focus on:

Brainstorming			Researching			Outlining

Character Sketch		Setting				Dialoge

Scene(s)			POV				Plot

Revisions/Edits			Synopsis			Pitch

Other: _____

Writers on Task

Today I will focus on:

Brainstorming   Researching   Outlining

Character Sketch   Setting   Dialoge

Scene(s)   POV   Plot

Revisions/Edits   Synopsis   Pitch

Other: _____

Writers on Task

Today I will focus on:

Brainstorming Researching Outlining

Character Sketch Setting Dialoge

Scene(s) POV Plot

Revisions/Edits Synopsis Pitch

Other: _____

Writers on Task

Today I will focus on:

Brainstorming Researching Outlining

Character Sketch Setting Dialoge

Scene(s) POV Plot

Revisions/Edits Synopsis Pitch

Other: _____

Writers on Task

Today I will focus on:

Brainstorming   Researching   Outlining

Character Sketch   Setting   Dialoge

Scene(s)   POV   Plot

Revisions/Edits   Synopsis   Pitch

Other: _____

Writers on Task

Today I will focus on:

Brainstorming   Researching   Outlining

Character Sketch   Setting   Dialoge

Scene(s)   POV   Plot

Revisions/Edits   Synopsis   Pitch

Other: _____

Writers on Task

Today I will focus on:

Brainstorming				Researching				Outlining

Character Sketch			Setting					Dialoge

Scene(s)					POV						Plot

Revisions/Edits				Synopsis				Pitch

Other: _____

Writers on Task

Today I will focus on:

Brainstorming   Researching   Outlining

Character Sketch   Setting   Dialoge

Scene(s)   POV   Plot

Revisions/Edits   Synopsis   Pitch

Other: _____

www.ingramcontent.com/pod-product-compliance
Lightning Source LLC
Chambersburg PA
CBHW080024110526
44587CB00022BA/3885